DORAEMON™
Gadget Cat from the Future

Hello!

I am DORAEMON

VOLUME **1**

Fujiko F. Fujio PRESENTS

A cat-shaped robot
born on September 3, 2112.
He rode a time machine all the way back from
the 22nd century to help Nobita.
He can pull all sorts of secret tools out of
the "4-D(Fourth Dimensional) Pocket"
on his tummy whenever Nobita needs them
to get himself out of trouble.

3

藤子・F・不二雄

Contents
もくじ

Guide to the Book
この本の読み方

「ワッ」の英訳。おどろきの声や効果音は、アメリカのまんが的な表現を使用したり、音のひびきを英語で表したりして、ふん囲気を出しています。英語辞書にのっていないものも、あります。

原作のまんがに合わせ、右開きですので、ふきだしは、右から左へと読んでください。

てんとう虫コミックス「ドラえもん」のまんがのセリフが、そのままついています。

気にさわったかしら.

ぼくだけど.

WAH!

Did I upset you?

It's me.

おどろきの声や効果音は絵としてあつかっていますので、そのまま訳さずのせています。

ドラえもんのひみつ道具は、日本語部分では「」（かっこ）をつけています。

きみにもつけてやる.

「タケコプター」

I'll put it on for you.

"Take Copter"

まんがのセリフを英訳。特に意味を重視しながら訳しているので、原文には出てこない単語が英訳に出てくる場合があります。

ドラえもんのひみつ道具は、英語部分では""（クオーテーションマーク）で表しています。原則として、ひみつ道具は斜体のローマ字で表していますが、外来語として定着している単語（クリーム、カメラ、ペンシルなど）は、英語で表示しました。

I'm glad you understood.

Thank you, thank you.

DORAEMON

Gadget Cat from the Future

All the way from the future

未来の国からはるばると

K-KLONG K-BONG K-KLONG

いやあ、ろくな ことがないね。

今年はいいことが ありそうだ。　のどかなお正月 だなあ。

野比（のび）のび太は 30分後に首をつる。

出てこいっ。　だれだ、へんな こというやつは。

40分後には 火あぶりになる。

KLAM KLATTA KLAM

気持ち悪いなあ。　……だれもいない。

今日からドラえもんがめんどう見るよ.

ドラえもんに話はきいたろ.

He's going to take care of you from today.

I think Doraemon told you.

あれっドラえもんは？

Oh, where's Doraemon?

おじいさんはなにをやらせてもだめなんだもの.

My grandpa can't do anything right.

あいつもできのいいロボットじゃないけど, おじいさんよりはましだろ.

He's not a well-made robot, but he's better than my grandpa.

ぼくがついてればいいんだけど, いそがしいもんでね,

I wish I could, but I'm busy.

でも, これからはドラえもんがついてるから安心しな, おじいさん.

But don't worry. From now on, Draemon'll be with you, Grandpa.

だから, おとなになっても, ろくなめにあわないんだ.

So he'll be still unlucky when he grows up.

勉強もだめ, スポーツもだめ, じゃんけんさえ勝ったことがない.

He does badly in school, doesn't like sports, and he even never wins at "rock, scissors, paper".

ドラえもんにきかなかったの？

Didn't Doraemon tell you about that?

やあ, ごめん.

Hey, sorry.

だれのこと？

Who?

ちょっと待てよ. おじいさん, おじいさんてだれのこと.

Hold on a minute. Who's Grandpa?

セワシくんはのび太くんの まごのまごなんだ.

なんの こと？

「タイムマシン」できたら， 出口がつくえの中に ひらいちゃってね.

ぼくらは未来の 世界の者だ.

な.

頭悪いな.

ぼくはまだ子どもだぞ. 子どもにまごが あるもんか.

だから，きみは ぼくのおじいさん のおじいさん.

ほんとか!?

もらうんだよ， 19年後に

そうかしら.

そしたらおよめさ んをもらうだろ.

あのね……，きみ だっていつかは おとなになるだろう.

ジャイアン の妹の？

ジャイ子!?

ジャイ子とか いったっけな.

あ，相手はだれ？ しずちゃんじゃない？

どうした.

What happened?

WAP WAP
WAP

バババン

そんなでたらめ
信じないぞ.

I don't
believe
you.

こんなとこから，人が
出るわけないだろう，
アハハハハ.

People came out
of here? That's
impossible,
a, ha, ha, ha, ha.

こわいゆめを見たのね.
かわいそうに，おお，
よしよし.

You had a
horrible
dream.
There, there,
dear.

のび太ちゃん!!

Nobita-chan!!

しかしたいした
空想力だ.

But really, his
imagination
is something.

よけいな心配しないで，
のびのびと育ってね.

Don't
worry. Take
it easy.

のび太はきっとしあ
わせになれるよ.

I'm sure
Nobita'll have
a happy life.

14

だけど……,
ほんとにゆめかな.

まんが家になれば,
成功するかもしれんぞ.

> But..., was that really a dream?

> He might succeed as a cartoonist.

つりたくない者が,
つるわけない.

つりたくない.

あと1分しかない.

30分後に
首つり.

> So it can't be true.

> No, I don't.

> Do I want to hang myself?

> There's only 1 minute left.

> He said I'd hang myself in 30 minutes.

いま, ぼくは首
をつりたいか？

これではっきりした.

> Hi, Shizu-chan.

> Nobita-san.

> It's all clear.

> That was nonsense, just as I thought.

やあ, しずちゃん.

のび太さあん.

やっぱりでたらめだ.

よ, よ,
よしきた.

ハネを取って.

> Oh..., OK.

> Reach that shuttlecock for us.

まあっ!! しつれいしちゃう.

Oh, you're so rude!!

おまえなんか, ぜったいにもらってやらないからな!!

I'll never marry a girl like you!!

こんなまっくろにしなくてもいいだろ.

You've gone too far.

ブジョクされたあ.

He insulted me.

だれだ, ジャイ子をなかしたのは.

Who made Jaiko cry?

SLOOP

そればっかりはないでしょう.

that could happen to me.

いくらなんでも…,

There's no way...

40分後に火あぶり…….

I'll be burned alive in 40 minutes...

キャッ, 早くきがえなさい.

Oh! Hurry up and change your clothes.

SHAPS

なにいってるの.

これも一種の火あぶり……. あたった.

What are you talking about?

I'm sort of burning myself... They're right.

1979年…….

こ，こ，これには ぼくの未来が うつっている.

In 1979...

Th, th, this is my future.

1988年 しゅうしょくできなくて 自分で会社をはじめ記念

くじけるな

来年もあるぞ

七転び

入学試らくだい なぐさめパーティー

1995年 会社つぶれ 借金取りおしかけ記念

1993年 会社丸やけ記念

花火

18

歴史の流れが変わっても、けっきょくぼくは生まれてくるよ。

心配はいらない。ほかでつりあいとるから。

ぼくの運命が変わったら、きみは生まれてこないことになるぜ。

だけど、どれを選んでも、方角さえ正しければ大阪へつけるんだ。

たとえば、きみが大阪へ行くとする。いろんな乗りものや道すじがある。

わかってくれて、よかった。

よろしく、よろしく。

めんどう見てやるよ。

このドラえもんがつきっきりで…、

じゃ、これでまわろう。

早く帰らないと、ママがうるさいぜ。

せっかくきたんだ、20世紀の町を見物したいな。

てんとう虫コミックス「ドラえもん」
第1巻 収録作品

Buy some sweets

for our guest right away.

いそいで、なにかおかしを買ってきて.

What a pain!

めんどくさいなあ.

Dora-emon.

Go shop-ping.

お使いだぞ.

ドラえもん.

Oh, he isn't here.

あれっ、いないのか.

22

PAK

カパ

"*Henshin Crackers*"

へんしん
変身
ビスケット

動物ビスケットか.

Animal crackers.

これでいいや.

They'll do.

パク

POP

お待ちどおさま.

Here you go.

23

もっと，ちゃんとしたおか
しを買ってらっしゃい!!

Buy some proper sweets for him!!

いえ，ビスケットなら，
わたし大好きです．

That's OK. I love them.

なんですか，ビス
ケットなんか．

Why did you choose crackers?

?

?

これとこれと
……．

ニャン．

Meow.

This one, and this one...

まちがいニャい．

OK.

ヒイフウミイ…．

One, two, three...

はい，おつり．

Here's your change.

人の顔じろ
じろ見て．

Don't stare at me.

いやだなあ，

Oh, gross!

こ，これがぼくの顔!?

Is this my face!?

!

えっ，
あのビスケットを!!

助けてくれえ． ドラえも〜ん．

What! You ate the crackers?!

Help me! **Doraemon.**

食べて少したってから，
ききめが出てくる．

ほ，ぼくは
どうなるの．

「動物変身ビスケット」だぞ．あんな
ものかってに食べるやつがあるか．

You eat the crackers, and in a little bit it takes effect.

What's happening to me?

They're "Doubutsu Henshin Crackers". Why did you eat the cracker without asking me?

よかった．

Thank goodness!

You'll return to yourself in about 5 minutes.

BOP

5分ぐらいで，
もとにもどるけどね．

25

わからない. 食べたかしら. ママに しかられる. お客に食べさせたとは, やっかいなことを….

I don't know.

Did he eat them?

Mom'll scold me.

If he ate any, we'll be in trouble.

からだに 変わりない? ひい, ふう, みい, …… ああっ, 4個も食べてる, いやしんぼ. 食べた? その ビスケット.

You don't feel changed, do you?

One, two, three..., oh, no, you ate four of them. What a pig!

Did you eat the crackers?

TMP TMP

ないんだよ. ききめをとめる 方法はないの? なんですかっ, しつれいな!!

No.

Isn't there a way to stop the effect?

Stop that. You're so rude!!

ウマ型のききめが, あらわれかけてる. ?! **WHEE-HEE HEE** **HA HA HA**

It's transforming him into a horse.

?!

だいじな話.

I have something important to talk about.

お客さん, ちょっとちょっと.

Excuse me, sir.

シッ.

Shh!

ごゆっくり, きき めがきえるまで.

Take your time until the effects wear off.

どうも.

Thanks.

ここが, トイレです.

This is the bath-room.

あ, もうきえましたね. 帰ってよろしい.

Oh, the effects have worn off. You can go back to the room.

げんかんに ある.

I put them at the door.

のびちゃん, おかしは?

Nobi-chan, where are the sweets?

ケッコウケッコウ.

Cock-a-doodle-doo.

いや, これはけっこうな おかしを.

Oh, thank you for the nice sweets.

お口に合いませんで しょうが…….

I hope you like it.

また トイレへ.　　お客さん.　　つぎはニワトリ型だ.

電話ですよ.　　なんとか しなくちゃ.　　いいかげんに しなさい！

ハイハイ，どなた？　　もうすぐかかってくるの.

さっぱり わからん！　　え？…… なんだって？　　なんの話？　　お話しましょうよ，1時間ほど.　　エへへ，べつにその，どなたってほどのものでもないけど.

やれやれ.

BOP

Thank goodness.

あ, まだききめが…….

だれかのいたずらだ. トサカにくる!

Oh, it's still in effect...

Somebody tricked me. I'm upset!

EEE EE EE **HA HA HA**

WAH! WAH!

見ちゃだめ!

Don't look at him!

あら, そう ですか.

そろそろ, おいとまします.

Please forgive me for not being more hospitable.

Oh, do you?

Well, I guess I'll be leaving.

おかまいも しませんで.

お客さまに, なんですか. ゆるしませんよ!!

Behaving like this to our guest is unforgivable!

CROAK
CROAK いいや，カエル！

No, I'll go home.

あと1個 のこってるのに． もうしばらく いたら？

There's one more effect left.

Why not stay a little longer?

あっ，パパ． ただいま．

There's Dad.

I'm home.

足がすくんで 入れない． ママ，おこってる だろうな．

I'm too scared to step into the house.

Mom'll be angry with us.

あっ，つまみ食い したな．

Oh, you sneaked a cracker!

なんだ，またなにか やったのか．

Hey, don't tell me you two are in trouble again?

I'll apologize to her for you.

てんとう虫コミックス「ドラえもん」第1巻 収録作品

ぼくがママに あやまってやるよ．

Hello, who is this?

Shadow hunting
かげがり

Hey, weed the garden.

おうい、庭の草をむしりなさい。

33

そんなものない. 草むしり機出してよ.

I don't have anything like that.

Give me a weeding machine.

あたりまえだ. おこった.

He should be.

He's upset.

ぼくは, ほんとうの子じゃないんだ. わかった！

I'm not his real son.

Hey!

おとうさんは, 自分の子どもが, かわいくないのだろうか.

I wonder if my father doesn't love his own son.

こんな日に外へ出たら, 日射(にっしゃ)病になるぞ.

If I go outside in this heat, I'll get sunstroke.

やれやれ, あれを出すか.

OK, I'll give you that.

なにをくだらない. ああ, ぼくのほんとうの親は, どこにいるのだろう.

Don't be ridi-culous.

Oh, where is my real dad?

このへん？ 日あたりのいいところに立って.

Like here?

Stand somewhere sunny.

30分あれば, じゅうぶんだよ. 草むしりくらい. ただし, 30分だけ.

That's enough time to weed.

But only for 30 minutes.

34

SHUFFLE, SHUFFLE

ムクムク

?

チョキチョキ

SNIP SNIP

動かないで.

Don't move.

PKK, PKK

ゼゼゼゼ

30分以内に, 庭の草をむしれ.

か, かげが 動き出した.

Weed the garden within 30 minutes.

My shadow is moving!

30分だよ.

For only 30 min-utes!

Now I can relax and take a nap.

安心して, ひるねができる.

おお, まっくろになって はたらいているな.

よし, よし.

Good for you.

Oh, you're working so hard!

30分たったら, このso りで くっつけないと, たいへんな ことになるよ.

わかったよ!

OK! I under-stand.

Something terrible will happen if you don't stick the shadow with this glue in 30 minutes.

のどがかわいた．コーラ
を持ってきてくれ．

え，もう終わった？10分
しかたっていないのに．

I'm thirsty. Get me a coke.

What? You've finished already? It's only been 10 minutes.

自分で自分を使うんだから，
えんりょがいらないや．

あおげ．

Since it's me ordering myself around, I can do whatever I like.

Fan me!

のび太くんを
おねがいします．

ちがうの？

もしもし，
のび太くん？

May I speak to Nobita?

It isn't?

Hello. Nobita?

The phone is ringing.

電話だぞ．

すぐとどけ
させるよ．

ごめん，ごめん，
長くなって．

あ，きみに
借りてた本ね．

しゃべれないの？

なんかいったらどう!?

He'll bring it to you right away.

Sorry it has been so long.

Oh, the book I borrowed from you.

You can't speak?

Why don't you say something!?

36

あっ, もうすぐ30分たつのか.

Oh, it's been almost 30 minutes.

ごくろうさん.

Thanks.

近所だから, もうすぐ帰るよ.

He's in the neighbor-hood, he'll be back soon.

なんてことを!!

What were you thinking!?

お使いに出した!?

You sent him on an er-rand!?

ま, 5分や10分, いいじゃないの.

Well, what difference can 5 or 10 minutes make?

なんだよ, 大げさな.

What are you talking about!?

こりゃあ…, ひょっとして手おくれかも…….

Oh no, it might be too late...

帰らないじゃないか. **FIDGETING**

He's not back yet.

ええっ.

What!?

しまいには, あいつがほんものになって, きみがかげにされちゃうぞ.

In the end, he'll become Nobita and you'll become a sha-dow!

時間がたつと, あいつはだんだんちえがついて, かげのままでいるのが, ばからしくなってくるぞ.

As time passes, the shadow will get smarter and smarter, he'll start to think it's silly to stay a shadow!

いまのうちに，くっつ
けないと……．

We have to stick
him to you at
once...

おやつにしましょう．　のび太さん，ドラちゃん．

Snack
time!

Nobita,
Dora-
chan.

えっ，とっくに帰ったって．

He left a long
time ago!?

SWISH

２時間もあれば，ひとりでにかげ
いやだあ．　とほんものが，入れかわるからな．

Oh, no!

If two hours go by, you
and the shadow will
switch automatically.

どこかへかくれて，時間の
たつのを待ってるんだ．

He's hiding somewhere
and waiting for
time to pass.

このさい，すいかなんかどうでもいい．

ずるい！ぼくのいないときに食べて．

あっ．

いいえ，さっきのかげは，たしかにあなたの…．

と，とんでもない．ぼく，食べてないよ．

SPIN

キャ．

わけはあとで．

やっぱり，家の中にいるんだ．

SHIVER

もう，かげになりはじめたぞ！

きみだよ!!うす黒くなってきている．

なになに，なにがどうしたの？

どこへ行ったんだろう.

Where is he?

わあ, 口を
きくよ.

Hey, he can talk.

イヤダネ.

No way.

もとどおり, のび太
くんにくっつくんだ.

Stick your-self to Nobita!

GRIN

SLIP

We'll catch you!

よおし!

かげをつかまえるには,
「かげとりもち」
がいるんだ.

We need "Kagetori-mochi" to catch a shadow.

BANG

SWISH

ぼくはこっち. ぼくは，こっちを さがす.

I'll go this way.

Then I'll go this way.

ペッペッ，どろ水だ.

Pe, pe, it's muddy water.

SPLASH

こっちがかげか.

So that's the shadow!

うぬっ.

OK.

えっ，ほんもの？

Nobita?

ケケケッ

CRASH

Ke, ke, ke.

41

あとで, ゆっくりしかられるから. のび太!

You can take your time scolding me later.

Nobita!

いやだなあ. さっきより, ずっとかげに近づいている.

Oh, no.

You're even more shadowy!

SPLASH

SWISH 天じょううらへかくれるぞ.

He's trying to hide in the attic.

モウスグ入レカワレルゾ.

We'll switch soon!

なんとかして! もうすぐ時間がきれる.

Do something!

We're running out of time.

かげに暗い所へ入られちゃ, おしまいだよ. なにも見えない.

That's it. We can't find a shadow in the dark.

We can't see anything.

I got it!

JUMP

You can't run away any more.

I won't forgive you, Doraemon.

Scold him in a sunny place.

とうとうつかまえた. のび太くんのかげなら,
ママのかげにはよわいだろうからね.

We've finally caught him. Nobita's shadow is weaker than his mom's shadow.

SNIP SNIP

チョ チョ
キ キ

ヌウ

Give me a hand.

たのむ.

LOOM

Then I'll go this way.

I'll go this way.

I want to get a perfect score once in my life...

一生に一度は百点を

いつものとおり100点だよ.

You got 100 as usual.

のび太くん.

Nobita-kun.

きのうのテストの答案をかえします.

I'll return the yesterday's papers.

どうしても100点以上取れない.

I can't get more than 100.

くやしいなあ.

That's strange.

ほかの者も,見習いなさい.

We should all learn from his example.

きみは, どうしてそんなによくできるんだろう.

How is it he's so good?

あれが, ひょうばんの天才少年よ. すてきねえ.

That's the boy genius everybody is talking about. He's nice.

のび太さんて, すごいわねえ.

You're great, Nobita.

宿題
終わったかい.

Have you finished your homework?

HEH HEH HEH SIGH!

UH

学園祭の打ち合わせ
があるんだぞ.

You've got a school festival planning meeting.

しずちゃんとこへ
行く約束だろ.

You were supposed to go to the Shizu-chan's house.

さっきからなに
やってたんだ!!

What have you been doing?

WILL YOU BE QUIET?!

そんなものさっさと
かたづければいい
のに.

You should finish it quickly.

悪いと
思わないの.

Don't you feel badly?

きっと, もうみんな
待ってるよ.

Everybody's probably waiting for you.

NAG NAG

なにも, そうヤクに
ならなくても…….

Don't be ridiculous...

ドラえもんだけ,
行けばいいじゃないか.

Why don't you go by yourself?

どうせ, ぼくは
頭が悪いからね.

After all, I'm a fool.

てまどって
悪かったな!

I know I'm slow!

SKRITCH SKRITCH
SKRITCH SKRITCH

かえせよ.

さあ，しずちゃんとこへ行こう.

「コンピューターペンシル」だよ.

あっというまにできた.

行こうよ，学園祭の打ち合わせに.

あれ，まだいたの.

おもしろいから.

もうちょっとかせよ.

SKRITCH SKRITCH SKRITCH

近ごろの宿題は，むずかしくて りょうが多いだろ．なかなか かたづかなくて．

We have lots of difficult homework these days. It takes so long to finish.

かしな． じつは，まだ 宿題が……．

Give it to me.

Actually, I'm still doing my homework...

いいから， いいから．

おまえ，いつからそんなに 頭がよくなった？

Never mind.

Since when have you got so smart?

それがねえ． きたよ．

Actually...

Hi.

なんか あるんだよ． あのバカが きゅうに…． おかしい!!

He must have some secret.

That Nobita...

That's strange !!

家で，さわいじゃ いけませんて．

パパが お仕事してるの．

Dad's working here.

So we've got to be quiet in the house.

48

SKRITCH SKRITCH
SKRITCH SKRITCH

ちょっとしつれい.

Excuse me, sir.

これすべて, 日ごろの努力が実をむすんだのです.

This is the fruit of my everyday efforts.

I've been studying hard while you were sleeping.

しょくんがねているまも, ぼくはせっせと勉強にはげんだからなあ.

そんなら, おれたちにもよこせ.

なにかいいくすりでもあったのか.

いったいどうしたの.

If so, give it to us.

Do you have some amazing drug?

What is it?

What are you talking about! How dare you?

なにをいうんだ, しつれいな!

ほんとかなあ.

まじめにやれば, かならずぼくのようになれるよ.

しょくんも, あきらめることないよ.

Are you sure?

If you study hard, you're sure to be like me.

So you shouldn't give up.

あしたテストが
あるんだ.

まだ
借りとくよ.

We'll have a test tomorrow.

I'm going to use it for a while.

もういいだろ,
かえせよ.

ああいい気持ち.

That's enough. Give it back to me.

I feel great.

いいじゃない. いっぺんぐらい,
100点取ってみたいよ.

Hey, I want to get a perfect score at least once in my life.

ずるい!!
それじゃカンニングと同じだ!

That's not fair!! It's virtually cheating!

ほしいものは手に入れるのが
おれのやりかたさ.

I get whatever I want. That's just my way.

おれもほしい
なあ….

いいなあ.

I want it, too.

Sure would be nice.

あのエンピツの
おかげか.

なるほど
なるほど.

He used that pencil.

I see.

あなた!!へんなこと約
束しちゃこまります.

それから, のび太のほしがってた
ものはなんでも買ってやろう.
なんでもかんでも.

Oh, darling!! Don't promise him such things.

And I'll buy you whatever you want. Anything!

ようし, 冬休みには世界一
周旅行につれていこう.

OK, I'll take you on a round-the-world trip during winter vacation.

50

ところがあるんだな，
このエンピツさえあれば．

But it's possible, because I have this pencil.

ハハハ，通信ぼが，オール5だったらという
話さ．そんなこと，ありっこないじゃないか．

Ha, ha, ha, I'll keep my promise if he gets straight A's in his report card. That's impossible.

PHEW!

フン．

HMPH!

ドラえもん，きみも
つれてってやるからね．

Doraemon, I'll take you on the trip with us.

きたないものでも
見るような……．

Like I was a cheater or something.

けいべつしきった
ような目つき……．

That look of contempt...

あの目……．

That look...

あしたはぜったいに
使ってやるぞ!!

I'll definitely use it tomorrow!!

…………
かまうもんか!!

... I don't care!!

51

B-BMP B-BMP B-BMP

では
はじめ!

答案用紙は行き
わたったかね.

Then, start!

Does everybody have an answer sheet?

ふつうのエン
ピツでやろう.

やめた!

I'll use a normal pencil.

I won't use it!

えらい!

かえすよ,
使わなかった.

あれじゃあ,
0点かもしれないな.

Good for you!

Here it is. I didn't use it.

I'm afraid I'll get zero on the test.

どこで入れかわ
ったんだろう?

へんだなあ.

ふつうのエンピツに
手を加えただけの
ニセモノだぞ.

When could it have gotten switched?

That's strange.

It's an imitation. It's just an ordinary pencil.

あれ…, これちがうよ.

Hey, this isn't my pencil.

さては! おれだけ100点! 見ろ、見ろ.

こんどのテストは
むずかしかったので,
みんな成せきがよくなかった.

なくほど
うれしいのかい. とうちゃん.

なんのことだ.
知らないな.

「コンピューターペン
シル」かえせっ!

100点なんか
こりごりだい!!

いつも落第点のおまえが, きゅ
うに100点取れるわけがないっ.

てんとう虫コミックス「ドラえもん」第1巻 収録作品

できの悪いのはしかたがない
として, 不正だけはするなと
教えてきたはずだぞ!

53

Hot snow

いま行くよう.

I'm coming.

遊びに行こう.

Let's go play.

のび太さあん.

Nobita～a.

外はさむいんだもの. だってえ,

It's cold outside.

Well...

ブルブル

SHIVER SHIVER

なんてかっこうだ.

What's that get-up!

あきれたあ. ゆたんぽ.

What a guy!

A hot-water bottle!

THUD

ガシャ

おれなんか, シャツも
きてないぞ.

I'm not even wearing an undershirt.

ぼくなんかこの下は,
シャツ1まいだ.

I'm only wearing a shirt under this.

なによ, これぐらいのさむさ.

It's not so cold.

55

ぼくたちは強いなあ.　We're tough.

のび太は
よわむしだなあ.　Nobita is a wimp.

なんだい, そのかっこう.　What's that get-up!

ばかにされた.　I look stupid.　**DARN IT!**

Doraemon.

ドラえもおん.

みんなが
いうんだ.　Every-body says so.

よわむしだと.　A wimp?

なにっ.　What!

それがどう
した.　What's up?

ぼくはもともと
さむがりなんだ.　I get cold easily.

みんなを，あっと，いわせよう．

We'll give them a shock.

よおしよおし．

OK. OK.

くやしいよ，きみの力で，なんとかならないか．

I feel awful. Can't you do anything?

DAB DAB

ほんのちょっぴりぬればいい．

Use just a little.

「あべこべクリーム」

"Abekobe Cream".

Brrr... **SHIVER SHIVER**

こたつに入ってみな．

Get under the kota-tsu.

あれえっ，なんだかあたたかくなってきた．

Hey, I'm getting warmer.

このクリームをぬると，熱いものにさわると，つめたく感じるんだ．そして，さむいときは，あたたかく感じるんだよ．

This cream makes you feel cold when you touch something hot. And when it's cold, you feel warm.

つめたあい．まるで，れいぞうこみたい．

It's cold! Like a refrigerator.

あたたかあい.

へやいっぱいに北風を入れよう.

It's warm.

Let the north wind fill the room.

WHISTLE

だから,「あべこベク リーム」というんだ.

WHISTLE

ぬげばぬぐほど, あたたかくなる.

こんなのぬいじゃえ.

That's why it's called "*Abekobe* Cream".

The more I take off, the warmer I feel.

I don't need these.

WHISTLE

のび太さん!

海水よくに行こう.

夏みたいだ.

Nobita!

Let's go swimming in the sea.

It's like summer.

LOOK!

このあついのに, よくそんな あつぎでいられるなあ.

やあ, みんな.

How can you be wearing such heavy clothes on a hot day like this?

Hi, guys.

おかしくなったんだ.

You're crazy.

やせがまんだろ.

You're just pretending, right?

ほんとに. さむくないの.

Are you sure?

Aren't you cold?

なんだと. きみたちは，よわいなあ.
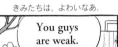
What!?

You guys are weak.

ぼくは，強いからね.

It's because I'm tough.

TOSS TOSS

ぼくだって.

Me too!

そのぐらい，おれだって.
OK, I'll take off my clothes.

SHIVER SHIVER WHISTLE
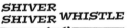

どうだ，まいったか.

How's this? Look at us.

59

と，とてもがま
んできない.

AHCHOO　AHCHOO

I can't
take it.

ハクション　ハクション

**GIGGLE
GIGGLE**

ふだんから，からだをきたえ，
食べものも好ききらいせず….

それは
もちろん.

どうして，そんな
に強くなったの.

I usually do some body building, and I
don't have any likes and
dislikes in food...

クスス

Well...

How did
you get that
strong?

DRIP

あら，雪だわ.

FALL

ポト

It's
snowing!

チラリ

へんなの.

やけどするう.

あち，あち.

It's hot!!

That's
strange.

We'll get
burned.

Ouch,
ouch!

アチイッ

60

やけどするっていうから，水をかけて，

They say they'll get burned, so let's throw water on them and...

Cool them down.

ひやしてやろう．

わかんないけど．

I don't know.

どうしたんだろう．

What happened?

SPLASH

それっ．

There!

氷みたいな水だぜ．

The water is ice cold!

ゆでだこにする気かっ．

You want us to be boiled octopuses?

Ow, ow, ow, ow!!

熱いおふろに入ってひやそう．

Let's take a hot bath and cool down.

「あべこべクリーム」を，ぬってるから，ひやそうと思えば，あっためなくちゃ．

We put on "*Abekobe* Cream", so we have to warm ourselves if we want to cool us down.

つけっぱなしでわすれてたわ.
きっと, わきすぎよ.

あらっ,
たいへん.

おふろがわいて
るかって.

I forgot to turn off the gas. I'm sure it's too hot.

Oh, no!

You want to know if the bath is ready?

なにいってんの.

SPLASH

What are you talking about?

It's cold!!

そんなひまないや

うめなきゃ入れないわ.

We don't have time.

Pour some water in.

つめたあい.

きゃあっ, こおってる.

Eek, they're frozen!

I can't take a test without "*Anki-pan*"

テストにアンキパン

どうしよう． **WHRR WHRR** こまった．
こまった．

どう考えても　　　う〜ん……．
わからない．

やかんとまくらを　　あしたテストがあるんだ．　　　　　　　さっきから，なにを
もってるのは？　　　国語と算数といっぺんに．　　　　　　　こまっているの．

こまった．こまった．　　まるでかんけいないけど，つまり，
　　　　　　　　　　　　それほどあわててるってこと．

こんなにこまって
みせてるのに.

おい，助けてくれ
ないのか！！

なあんだ.

See how much trouble I'm in?

Hey, won't you help me?

So I've heard.

やっぱりドラえ
もんはたよりに
なるなあ.

助けてくれるの.

それじゃ，この
せん風機で….

このままだと，かくじつに
0点をとっちゃうよっ.

You're reliable, just as I thought.

So you will help me?

Alright. This fan ...

If I take the test like this, it's certain I'll get a zero.

まじめに考え
てくれっ.

じゃ，この「動物ライト」
で先生をゴリラに…….

そんならんぼうな！！

学校をふきとばせば，
テストがない.

Will you be serious?

Then, we'll change the teacher into a gorilla by using this "*Doubutsu* Light"...

That's excessive.

If we blew the school away, you couldn't take the tests.

こんどだけ
助けて.

これからはちゃんと，
勉強するから.

ふだん，勉強しないのが
いけないんだっ.

Help me just this once.

I promise you, from now on I'll study every day.

It's your fault for not studying every day.

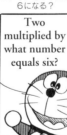

なにやってんだ!!

そうか，こないだはなをかむ
とき，ちり紙がなくて…….

……とおもったらかんじんの
ページがぬけてる.

Oh, what were you doing!!

That reminds me. The other day I was going to blow my nose, but I couldn't find tissues...

... but some important pages are missing.

ともだちのノートを
うつさせてもらう.

「アンキパン」を
うんとだしてよ.

I'll copy my friends' notes.

Give me lots of "Anki-pan".

とてもパンにうつして，
たべる気になれない.

ぼくは，よく
勉強するからな.

きたない
なあ.

I can hardly bring myself to copy it and eat.

You know, I study hard.

It's dirty.

おぼえることなら
自信があるんだ.

そんなかんたん
にいくなら
くろうしないわ.

さすがにしずちゃんのは
きれいだ. これをちょっと
おぼえちゃおう.

I'm confident about memorizing.

You're doing it so easily.

Shizu-chan's notebook is beautiful. I'll memorize it quickly.

ようしやってみせる．たとえばこの電話ちょうで…．

OK, I'll show you. For example, I'll use this phone book...

クラスでいちばんわすれんぼのあんたが？

HO HO HO

You're the most forgetful in the class!

はじめのほうのページなら，みんなおぼえた．

I memorized the first half of it perfectly.

?

FLIP FLIP GMPH MMPH

?

かるい，かるい．

すごい，ぴったりよ．

It's a piece of cake.

Gee! Perfect!

999の……！

柿久家子（かきくけこ）さんは？

999-...!

How about Kaki Kukeko?

１２３の４５６７

阿井上男（あいうえお）さんの番号は

123-4567.

What's the phone number of Ai Ueo?

おやつをどうぞ．

いいなあ．

テストで100点とるなんて，わけないね．

Have some sweets.

I envy you.

It's very easy to get a perfect score on the tests.

68

それじゃ,
ぼつぼつやるか.

まんがを見てたべてばかりいて,
勉強しないの？

おいしい草もち
だね. パクパク.

> Well then, I'll get to work.

> You do nothing but read comic books and eat. Don't you study?

> These mochi rice cakes are good. Munch, munch.

すこしおなかをへら
さないとだめだ.

GLAH　ウ…….

「アンキパン」を…….

ゲープ

> I have to let my stomach empty a little.

> Um...

> I put "Anki-pan" on...

たべたく
ない.

どこへいってた.
ごはんだぞ.

わるいけど,
ノートかして.

> I don't want to eat now.

> Where have you been? Dinner's ready.

> Sorry, but lend me your note-book, okay?

ゲープ.

とっても
おいしいわ.

母の日だからね.

おとうさんのつくったごはんを,
たべたくないというのかっ.

> BURP.

> It's delicious.

> It's Mother's Day.

> You mean you don't want to eat the meal your father made?

Have you memo-rized every-thing?

Not at all.

Oh, man...

I can't eat any more.

Um...

I borrowed the notebook, so I'll do it now.

I gave you lots of bread!!

GEH!

Wash it down with water.

I just can't eat it.

GUH...

Help me!

I'll make you eat all of them at any cost.

Do you want to get a zero?

I can't eat any more.

70

はやくでなさいっ.

Hurry up!

まあだだよ.

Not yet.

もういいかい.

Are you finished?

つぎの朝

THE NEXT DAY

おぼえたことをすっかり
だしちゃったな.

You must have lost everything you memorized.

たべすぎでおなかをこわした？まずいなあ.

He got a stomachache because of eating too much? That's bad.

えっ, のび太くんがトイレに1時間も！？

What? Nobita's been in the bathroom for an hour!?

勉強はつらいなあ.

Studying is so hard.

1ページめからたべなおしだ.

You have to eat again from page 1.

I can't get motivated.

It's always "study, study, study."

I was going to study a while ago, but...

Now that you've told me to, Mom, I don't want to.

Why can't you just trust me?

Then, do as you please.

OK, if I leave you alone, will you study voluntarily?

Of course!!

72

My birthday

ぼくの生まれた日

遊んでこよう.

I'll go out and play.

な，なにもあん
なにひどく…．

そ，それにしても….

しかたないよ．
わるいのはきみ
のほうだから．

There's no reason for them to be so harsh...

But...

That's too bad, but it's your own fault.

どこかでひろわ
れたんだ．

I must have been found somewhere.

ぼくはこの家の
ほんとの子じゃ
ないんだ．

なんの
こと？

I'm not their true son.

What are you talking about?

ひょっとしたら，そうだ！！
きっとそうなんだ！！

Maybe, so!! I'm sure it's true!!

ああ，ぼくのほんとのおかあさま！！
どこにいらっしゃるのかしら．

Oh, my true mother!! Where are you now?

ほんとの子なら，あんなひど
いおこりかたしないよ．

ハハハ，なにを
ばかな．

If I were really their son, they wouldn't be so angry at me.

Ha, ha, ha, don't be ridiculous!

どうして，今まで気が
つかなかったんだろ．

きみの生まれた
日へいこう．

Why didn't I think of that?

Let's go back to your birthday.

じゃあたしかめようよ，
「タイムマシン」で．

Then, let's make sure of it by "Time Machine".

74

10年前のぼくの家だ.

This is my house 10 years ago.

昭和39年8月7日でいいんだね.

On August 7 in the 39th year of Showa, right?

だれもいないよ.

Nobody's home.

But...

でも….

まだ, きずもらくがきもないね.

ここはとうさんのへやだったのか.

There aren't any scratches or marks so far.

This was my dad's room.

きっと病院だよ.

うそうそ!

WAAH

Probably they're at the hospital.

I'm kidding!

親がいなくて, どうしてぼくが生まれたんだ.

I'm afraid you were found somewhere just as you thought.

How could I be born without my parents?

やっぱりひろわれたのかねえ.

75

あっ, おとうさん.　　どこだ, どこだ.

TARUMP TARUMP

There's Dad.

Where's the baby?

まずいよ.　自分の子どもをわすれるとは.　えっ.　きみだれ？　やっぱり10年分わかいね.

Stop it!

How could you forget your own son!?

What!

Who are you?

He's ten years younger!

いや！そんなことより……,　なんだあれは.　？　きみはまだ, 生まれてないんだから.

Oh! Anyway...

Who are they?

?

You're not born yet.

会社を早びけしてきたんだよう.　電話をきいて,　生まれたというあかんぼうは, どこにいるんだ.

I left the office early.

I had a call, and...

Where's the newborn baby?

76

He's pretty confused.

Isn't he in the hospital?

Oh, you're right.

Maybe,

ああ, そうだっけ.

ひょっとして,

ぼくらもつれてってよ.

まってえ!

Let us go with you.

Wait!

ハッ, ごちそうさま, いや その……, どうも…….

男のお子さん ですよ.

Hh, thank you for the nice meal, oh, no..., thank you...

It's a baby boy.

HAFF HAFF

医院
産婦人科

Congratu-lations.

おめでとうございます.

きっと今のぼくににて, 玉の ようなかわいい子だよね.

どんな子か しら.

ぼくも.

ああ, どきどきするなあ.

ウフッ.

SPPLT!

I'm sure he's lovely just like me now.

I wonder what he's like.

Mine, too.

Oh, my heart's beating so fast.

おかあさん
そっくり.

大きいなあ！

He's just like his mother.

He's big!

おとうさんだよ.

BWAH!

I'm your daddy.

なんてまあ,
かあわいい.

WAAAW!

How lovely he is!

あかちゃんはそっちよ.

The baby's over there.

しわくちゃじゃんか,
まるでサルみたい！

His face is all wrinkled, just like a monkey!

ええっ,
これがぼく！?

What! Is this me!?

みせてみせて.

Show us!

生まれたてはあんなもんだよ.

Newborn babies are like that.

サルとはなんだっ.

A monkey? How dare you?

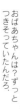
おばあちゃんは？ずっとつきそっていたんだろ.

あれ？

Where's my mother? She's been with you all the time?

Oh?

あんなしつけをした親の顔がみたい.

He's so rude. Imagine what his parents must be like.

さっきから，うろちょろしてるんだ.

He's been getting in my way for a while.

だれよあの子.

Who's that boy?

どんな名まえにする？

ところでこの子，

What do we name the baby?

By the way,

もう，顔じゅうくしゃくしゃにして….

よろこんでたろ.

Yeah, her face crumpled into a smile...

She must have been glad.

ご先ぞにほうこくするんだって，帰ったわ.あなたと入れちがいになったのね.

She went home to tell our ancestors about the baby, when you come.

もっとかっこいいい名に，してほしいや.

野比（のび）のび太！いい名だろ.

「のび太」

I wish I had a cooler name.

Nobi Nobita! Isn't it great!

Nobita.

ちゃんとね，考えてあるんだ.

I've already thought about it.

名まえの意味？もちろんあるよ.

The meaning of the name? Of course it means something.

また，どなられるぞ.

おい，よせ.

本人のきぼうもきいてくれるべきだ.

You'll be yelled again.

Hey, stop it!

They should ask me.

もう帰ろう.

We'd better go now.

いったいうちの子に，なんのうらみが！！

Is there any reason you have a grudge against my son!!

そんなたいした子じゃないんだから．いえほんと！

He's not much of a child. I'm serious!

ぼくのしょうらいを，あんなに楽しみにしてたのか.

They were looking forward to my future so much.

うん…………,

Yeah...

ほんとの子だってことはわかったろ.

You understood you're their true son, right?

どうしたんだ，急に勉強しだして.

It's strange that you've suddenly started studying. What happened?

からだをこわすから，もうねなさいってば.

You'll lose your health. Go to bed now.

82

A heavy snowslide in Nobita's room

勉強部屋の大なだれ

高いもんね，買ってくれないよね.

どうか，おとうさんが
買ってくれませんように.

だめだよねスキーは,

のび太がスポーツぎらいで，心ぱいしてたん
だよ. 自分でやる気になったとは感心だ.

なに，スキーを始めたくなった？
それはいいことだ.

うん……，よかった. よかったわね.

こんなこともあるか
と思って，ちゃんと
買っておいた.

で，でもさいわいいや，あいにく
雪がふらないとすべれない.

84

スキーができる。 ばんざい！ 天気予ほうです．まもなく雪がふるでしょう．

We can ski! Hooray! The weather forecast says we'll have snow soon.

なんとかしてっ！ ドラえもん‼

Help me! Doraemon!!

ふってからじゃ，手おくれなんだよ． ふってからやれば？

It'll be too late. Then, do it after it snows.

雪もないのにむりだい． スキーぐらい，練習すればいいよ．

I can't, because there's no snow. You should practice skiing.

あっ，なにか出してくれるの⁉ しようがないなあ．

Can't you give me something? Okay.

みんながぼくのころぶとこみょうと，待ってんだ．

Everybody will be looking forward to watching me fall down.

85

こうやってのるだろ

You stand on it just like this.

「おざしきゲレンデ」

"Ozashiki-Gerende"

なんだこれ？

What's this?

It starts moving.

すべりだすだろ.

いつまでもすべり続けられる.

You can keep skiing.

スピードにあわせてベルトが動くだろ.

The belt moves according to the speed.

とまるとベルトもとまる.

おもしろい、かして、

Looks fun, I wanna do it.

If you stop, the belt also stops.

ベルトもむきをかえる.

むきをかえると,

the belt turns with you.

If you change the direction,

FWIP 86

上にのるだろ.

I'm standing on it.

やっこらしょ……. さ, がんばって.

Here goes...

Let's do it.

ROLPP
ROLPP

ころがるスピードにあわせてベルトが動く.

The belt moves according to the rolling speed.

ころぶだろ.

SVOOP

I'm falling.

なんだ, もうやめるの !?

Hey, are you quitting it so soon!?

とまるとベルトもとまる.

If I stop, the belt also stops.

こんなとこでは, ばかばかしくてできない.

やれっ!

It's just too ridiculous to ski here.

Try again!

はじはかきたくないけど, いたいのはもっといやだ.

みんなの前ではじをかきたくないんだろ!

Of course I don't, but I hate pain.

You said you didn't want to feel humiliated in front of everybody!

よし，気ぶんを出してやる.

OK, I'll make such an atmosphere.

I don't feel like I'm skiing unless I'm actually on snow.

さあ練習を始めよう.　　「立体映画」をうつしたんだ.　　ああ，あれえつ！

Now, let's start practicing.

I used "3-D Movies".

What a surprise!

すべると，けしきも動いていく.

If you ski, the scene also moves.

ベルトはそのへんだ.

The belt is around there.

ころべば雪けむりもちゃんとうつる. **ROLL ROLL**

> If you fall down, a cloud of snow is projected.

また!! 気ぶんでないからやめる. この雪つめたくない.

> Again!!

> I don't feel like I'm skiing, so I quit.

> The snow isn't cold.

なるべくならこのボタン, 使いたくなかったのにな. ン……まあね. じゃ, なにかこの雪が冷たくて気ぶんが出れば, まじめに練習するのか?

> I'd rather not use this button.

> Well..., yes.

> You mean if the snow is cold, you feel like you're skiing, and you'll seriously practice?

KLIK

きみのためだぞ!! さむいよう. **SHIVER SHIVER**

> It's for you!!

> I'm cold.

> How is it? You've got the whole atmosphere now.

ど, どうだい気ぶん出たろ!

ぼくがとって
きてやる.

マフラーとって
くるんだよ.

にがすもんか!

I'll do it.

I'm going to get a scarf.

You won't escape!

さ, それまいてすべりな.

Now, wear it and ski.

そこがきみの悪い
ところだ!!

かんべんしてよ. もう,
スキーなんかいやなんだよ.

That's your problem!!

Let me go now. I don't wanna ski any more.

そんなことでは, いつまでたっても
なにもできないよ.

なにかやってみて, うまくいかない
とすぐいやになってしまう!

I guess you'll never accomplish anything.

If you do something and you can't do it well, you just give up!

HRR BRR
BRR HRR　　**A-CHOOO!**

KLIK

GROOHH　　　　**SWOOSS**
　　　　　　　　RMMBL

~~**HWOOO**　**RUMMM**　　**KRSSH**
　　　　　　　　　　　KRSSH

91

GROOOHH
いきすぎだっ!!

HWOOO

KLUDD!

こごえちゃう.
出口はどこだっ!

スキーどころじゃないっ.

~~GROH-H-H

おかしい!! なだれのしかけ
なんかないはずだ.

94

きょうは4月1日だから，
うそをついてもいいんだぞ.

> Today's April 1,
> so we can tell lies.

"*Usotsu-ki*"
うそつ機

4月1日？おまえ，なにをかんちがいしてんだ.

> April 1? What are
> you talking
> about?

えっ，きょうは4月2日？しまった…….

> What?
> Today's April
> 2? Gosh...

ということは，なぐられても
い，いえない.　もんくいえないな！

> I,
> I can't.

> That means you
> can't complain
> if you get
> punched!

ああっ，
だまされた.

べえ，
ほんとは4月1日だよ.

> Darn it!
> I was
> tricked.

> You fool!
> Actually, it's
> April 1.

やめとけ.

なんとかおかえししなきゃ,
気がすまない！

そのあと,スネ夫にも,しず
ちゃんにも,だまされて……．

You shouldn't.

I won't feel better unless I pay them back!

After that, I was tricked by Suneo and Shizu-chan...

どういういみ？

そこへいくと,
きみは……．

うそをつくには,
あるていど頭が
よくなくちゃ.

きみに,ひとをだませる
わけがないよ.

What do you mean?

That's why you ...

You have to be somewhat intelligent to lie.

You can't fool anyone.

いいものかすから,ゆるせ.

いいすぎた.
とりけす.

ごめん.

I'll lend you some good thing, so forgive me.

I've gone too far. I'll take back what I said.

Sorry.

えっ,うそを？

今から,きみに
うそをつく.

これを口に
かぶせて……．

「うそつ機」

What? A lie?

I'm going to lie to you.

I'll put it on my mouth...

"Usotsu-ki".

SAVE ME!

きみのうしろに
おばけがいる！

There's a
ghost behind
you!

これでうそをつけば，どんな
でたらめでも，本気にされる．

If you tell lies using
this, people will
believe anything.

つい，本気にしちゃ
った．ふしぎだな．

はじめに，うそだと
ことわっておいたのに…．

I took it
seriously in
spite of
myself.
Why?

I told you before-
hand that it was
going to be a lie...

勉強をすませてから，
遊びに行けというんだよ．

わかっていたら，
やりなさい．

That's
right.
Then,
study.

She's going to say
"You can go play
when you finish
studying".

うそつきに行こう．

Let's go to
tell lies.

Nobi-
chan.

のびちゃん．

なんですって？

ママはわたしです．あなたは，
のびちゃんじゃないの．

What are
you talking
about?

I'm your mom.
You're Nobi-
chan, right?

どうして，ママ
がやるのよ．

はやく勉強
しなさい．

Why do I
have to
study?

Start
studying
right
now.

97

さあ、みんなをだまして
やろう。

Now, let's go trick everybody.

ぼくは、なにをかんちがい
していたんだろう。　　そうだったのか。

I've guessed wrong.

He was right.

いた！　　　　　　　　　　いた！

AHAH!

AHAH!

あいつ、すぐに
ひっかかるから　　　もういちど、のび太
おもしろいや。　　　をだましてやろう。

It's fun, because he's easily taken in.

I'll trick Nobita again.

その火事がひろがって、
今もえているのはきみんちだぞ。

The fire spread, and now it's got your house.

のび太、なにやってんだ！
おまえの家が火事だぞっ。

Nobita, what are you doing! Your house is on fire.

勝った。

はやくにもつを
出さなきゃ！

火事だ、火事だ。

We've won.

We have to get our things out quickly.

Fire! Fire!

98

?

おまえは人間だ.
ひっぱってるほうが, 犬なんだ.

いくら4月ばかでも
やりすぎだ.

火星人がせめて
きたぞ.

なんでぼくが
ごはんを作るんだよ.

こんなにあっさりだまされ
ちゃ, おもしろみがないや.
もう, やめよう.

ママー,
ごはんまだ?

おなかすいたよ.

A dream town, Nobita Land

ゆめの町、ノビタランド

Make what?

Then, let's make it.

KLICK!

"Instant Construction Camera"

カシャ

Our own house.

SHWRR

It's done.

ポト

I'll develop the film.

PLUNK

But it's just a toy. It's useless.

Wow, it's just like a real house, even inside.

ここからはいるんだ.

We go in from here.

「ガリバートンネル」

"Gulliver Tunnel"

きみもトンネルをくぐれば,
この家に住めるよ.

If you pass through the tunnel, you can live in this house.

こっちこっち.

Here, here.

作ろう.

Let's make it.

いろんな家を写して,すきなように
町を作ることができる.

We can make our own town by taking pictures of various houses.

このカメラで写すものが,
なんでもそっくりもけいに
なるとすれば…….

If anything I take pictures of with this camera becomes a minia -ture...

本屋だね.

It's a book- store.

KLICK!

カシャ

かたっぱしから
とっちゃえ.

We'll go one by one.

柔原書店

104

おどろいた！

なにか，ちらばってる．

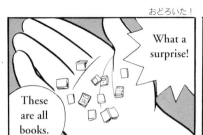 

これ，みんな本だよ．

豆つぶみたいなおかしがぎっしり．

じゃあ，おかし屋を写せば……．

えいが館，ボウリング場も，ほしいよ，写してこよう．

このへんを，大通りにしよう．

だけど，住んでる人は，どうなるの？

生き物は，写らないんだ．

きみたち，みんなの
ゆめをかなえて
あげよう．　しょくん．

I'll make your dreams come true.

Every-body.

のび太が，にやにやして
やってきたぞ．

Here comes Nobita, smirking.

HEH HEH

？　　？　　？

？　？　？

そんなとこあるもんか．
ねぼけるな．

ぼくたち
だけの町？

That can't be. Don't be silly!

Our own town?

へんなトンネルね．

Weird tunnel.

いいからいいから．

ここへはいれって？
からかうなよ．

Just try it.

We go in here? Stop joking.

TA-DAH!

KLUMBL

ラク

Hey! What happened?

わっ！なんだ.

みんな喜んでるよ. ここを
ノビタランドとよぼうって.

Everybody's happy. "Let's call this Nobita Land".

毎日, ここでまんがを
読もう.

Every day, I'll read comic books here.

じゃまっけねえ.

They're really in the way.

庭いっぱいおもちゃを
ならべて,

He put the toys all over the yard,

KLOTT

ズボ

ドラえもん, あき地を
作る機械をだして.

このへんに物置を建てて
くださいな.

土地だけは作れないなあ.

It's impossible to make land.

Doraemon, give me a machine which will make a vacant lot.

Please build a shed around here.

We can make
our own town by
taking pictures of
various houses.

Let's make it.

いばってやがんの！
たまに勉強してると思って．

Don't be so proud just because you're studying!

"Abekonbe"

アベコンベ

POIK

みろ！よけいなことという
から，まちがえた．

Look! I made mistakes because you said silly things.

WHA?!

RUBBA RUBBA

なにやったんだ.
やっぱりな. ろくな 使いみちないな.

What did you do?

Just as I thought. There's no good use for it.

I rubbed a notebook with an eraser, but it went all black!

消しゴムをかけたら, まっ黒になった！

POIK

さわったものが, あべこべにはたらくんだ.

これ, 「アベコンベ」.

チョン

It'll make things work in the exact opposite way.

This is "*Abekonbe*".

こんなのすてた ほうがいいや.

ねっ, とてもあつい かぜがでる.

I'd better throw it away.

See? A very hot wind is blowing out.

そうかな.

うまく使えば, きっと役にたつよ.

おもしろい じゃない.

ま, まて. もったいない.

I doubt it.

If we use it well, I'm sure it'll be useful.

It's fun.

Wait. What a waste!

さあ！さあ！ えっ？なにに使う？

Come on!

Hmm, what can we use it for?

さあ，なにに使う？

Now, how do we use it?

いろいろやってみれば，
そのうちいい使いみちがわかるさ.

If we try lots of things, we'll find a good use for it soon.

SPING!

KLOT　**KPOIK**　**KLOT**　　　　**KLOT**

SPSSH...

そろそろ，せんたくものが
かわいたころね.

It's about time the washing dried.

113

やっぱり，これはすてる
しかないかな．

I guess we'd better throw it away after all.

さかさに使ったら，もとへもどっ
た．さわぎはおさまったけど……．

They returned to normal when I used it upside down. The fuss was settled, but...

わからないなあ．

I don't get it.

これからやるよ．

I'll do it now.

いたずらばかりしてないで
宿題をすませなさい．

Don't play tricks all the time. Finish your homework.

すらすらとけるぞ．
おもしろくないっ．

I can solve them easily. It's no fun!

悪い頭なら，
よくなるはずだよ．

If you are stupid, it is sure to make you clever.

使いみちがみつかった！

I've found a use for it!

チョン

KOPP!

Moonlight and chirps

月の光と虫の声

CRE-EEE **CREE-EEE**

じゃあ, 声のききちん, 5円ずつ, いただきましょう.

Then, give me 5 yen for listening to them.

うっとりするよ.

I'm enraptured by them.

うん, ほんとにいい声だなあ.

Yeah, they sure do.

いい声だろう.

They chirp sweetly, don't they?

We need to pay to hear a bug's chirp?

虫の声をきくのに, お金がいるの.

CRE-E-E-E CREE CREE

だれがくるもんか.

Who would come back?

また, ききにおいで.

Come back to listen again.

デパートで買ってきたんだぞ. 高かったんだ.

I bought them at a department store. They were expensive.

むかしは，すず虫や，まつ虫なんか，家のまわりにいっぱいいたもんだ.

In the past, there were lots of crickets around houses.

買ってきても，すぐ死んじゃうからな.　うちでも買ってよ.

If we buy them, they'll die soon.

Buy some for me, too.

それが，どうしていなくなっちゃったの.

ほんと．夜になると，虫の音楽会でうるさいくらいだったわね.

Why do we rarely see them these days?

That's true. At night, their chirps were rather noisy.

つまんないの.

あき地が少なくなったし，くすりをまいたりしたから，虫たちがすみにくくなったのさ.

What a shame!

Because there are fewer vacant lots and we use insecticide, it's hard for them to survive.

うちの庭にはなそう.　すず虫や，まつ虫をうんととってこよう.

むかしの世界へ行こう.「タイムマシン」で.

And let them loose in our garden.

Let's catch lots of crickets.

Let's go back to the past by "Time Machine".

121

そんなに虫がいるもんか. ほんと？ 虫の音楽会を楽しませてあげる. 今夜，うちの庭においで.

There can't be that many crickets.

Really?

We can enjoy a chirping concert.

Come to our garden tonight.

20年ほどむかしへ行ってみよう.

Let's go back about 20 years ago.

いるかいないか，まあみてろ.

Let's see if there are or not.

KRUSSLE KRUSSLE

へえ，20年前はこんなにあき地があったんだね.

CREE CREE

CRE-E-E-E

Oh, there were so many vacant lots 20 years ago.

SKRUTTER RR-R-R RRRP SKRITTER

122

KRSSL KRSSL

CREE CREE CRE-EE

CREE CREE

虫の声で，いっぱいだ．

There's so much chirping.

KRS-S-S

CREEE R-R-RP RRP R-R-RP

楽しそうにうたってる．

They are chirping happily.

ひろびろとした草原で，月の光をあびて，

In the vast grasslands, bathing in moonlight,

すみにくい世界へつれていっちゃかわいそうだ．

It's cruel to take them to a world where it's hard for them to live.

ぼくも，そう思ったところだよ．

I was just thinking the exact same thing.

とってかえるの，よそうか．

Maybe we shouldn't take back any...

心配するな．いいものがある．

Don't worry. I'll give you something good.

虫をあつめてきたかい．あつめられるわけないよ．うそつきやあい．

Did you collect the crickets? You couldn't. You liar!

そのへんで, 虫をかきあつめよう.

Let's collect insects from the neighborhood.

この花のつゆをかけると, どんな虫でも きれいな声でなくんだよ.

If you drop the dew of this flower any insect, it will chirp beautifully.

こおろぎ, すず虫, まつ虫など, どっさりいるからね.

Lots of different kinds of crickets are in our yard.

やくそくどおり, 虫の音楽会をひらくよ.

As we promised, you can enjoy listening to chirps from now.

こんなにたくさん, どこで あつめたんだろう.

Where did they collect so many crickets?

Darn it!

みてろっ.

わあ, いいなあ.

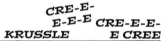

CRE-E-E-E-E
KRUSSLE
CRE-E-E-E CREE

Wow, that's great.

RUSSLE   KR-R-R KRR KRR

124

CREE CREE CREE

KRITTLE KRITTLE

ほんとにきれいな
なき声じゃ.

Their chirps are
really beautiful.

いいねえ.

That's
good.

あっ, それは.

Oh, no!

へへへっ,
虫はみんなもらったよ.

Hey,
I got all of your
crickets!

ZWOO-OOM!

SKITTER SKETTER

なんで,
ごきぶりなんかとってくるざます.

Why did you get
cockroaches?

SKEDDA SKIDDER

てんとう虫コミックス「ドラえもん」
第4巻 収録作品

125

126

"Ishikoro Boushi"

石ころぼうし

あぶないっ、おちたらどうするの！

> Watch out!
> It's
> dangerous.

FDGT FDGT

そのびんぼうゆすりのくせ、やめたほうがいいよ.

> You'd better get
> rid of the habit
> of shaking
> your
> legs.

もういやだ!

> I can't stand it!

赤んぼじゃ,
あるまいし.

ほっといて
ほしいな!

I'm not a baby.

Leave me alone!

それは, きみのことを
気にかけてるからだよ.

They care about you, that's all.

みんながぼくのこと見はっ
てて, うるさいこという!

Everyone watches me and scolds me!

かしてよ.
ねえ, ねえ.

そんなこと
いわずに,

けど……, よした
ほうがいいな.

Lend it to me.

Come on.

But..., you'd better not use it.

ないことも
ない.

ねえ, だれにも気に
されない機械って
ないかしら.

I have one.

Hey, don't you have a machine to help me?

?

いやちゃんと見えるんだけ
どね, 気にされなくなるの.

?

No. People see you. They just don't notice you.

それをかぶると, とう
明人間にでもなるの?

If I wear it, will I become, say, an invisible man?

「石ころぼうし」

"Ishikoro Boushi"

ちょっと
きついな.

SKWNK
SKWNK

It's a little bit tight.

そうか,
わかった.

たとえば, 道ばたに石ころがおちてるだろ.
でも, だれもそんなものに目をとめないだろ.

OK, I understood.

It's like a pebble on the side of the road. You may see it, but you don't really look at it.

どう？　にあう？なんだかへんじゃない？

What do you think?

How do I look?

Is this OK?

サイズはこれしかないんだ.

K-PUMP

サイズはこれしかないんだ.

I only have this size.

へんだなあ.

That's strange.

ドラえもん！

Doraemon!

へんじぐらいしろよ.

Talk to me!

目には見えても，まったく気にかからなくなったんだ！　ぼくはもう，石ころみたいになったのか.

People can see me, but they don't care about me at all!

I've already become like a pebble.

あっ，そうか.　どうしてひとりでにからだが，ゆれるんだろう.

I got it.

Why did my body sway all by itself ?

YIPPEE

どこで何をしても，だれにも，もんくいわれない！　ぼくは自由だ！

Nobody scolds me whatever I do, wherever I am!

I'm free!

SHLUMP

じゃ,
いってくる.

これから遊びに
いくけどいいね.

I'm going play from now on.

Good-bye.

おとうさん, ぼく
勉強やめたよ.

Dad, I quit studying.

ことしも大学入試に
失敗なさったの.

Did he fail the college entrance exams again this year?

おたくの
おぼっちゃんが?

まあ.

Your son?

Gee.

?

ど, どうも…….
しつれい.

?

I'm so sorry...

SNORT!

WAH HAH HA

ゲラゲラ

コチョ
コチョ

TICKLE TICKLE

130

道のまん中であぐらかいてても へいきなんだから.

I can sit cross-legged in the middle of the road.

いいなあ.

I feel great.

なんだ, うちへ かえるとこか.

Oh, she's going home.

やあ, どこへいくの？

Hi, where are you going?

はあい.

Yes, Mom.

しずちゃんおふろに はいりなさい.

Shizu-chan, take a bath.

よそのうちにどんどんあがっちゃう. ぼくは石ころなんだもん.

I can even go into her house, because I'm a pebble.

だめだなあ.

How cowardly!

ぼくって, 気が弱いなあ.

I'm timid.

かえろ.

I'll go home.

What? | That Nobita.

He's got zero sports talent. | He's slowpoke, stupid, and...

野球にさそわないで おこう. あいつを入れる と負けるから,

Let's not ask him to play baseball with us. | If he joins us, we'll lose the game.

ほくのせいじゃ ないよ. **KONK** ゴチ 気をつけろ.

THUDD!

I didn't do it! | Watch it!

きょうはへんに, むかむかする日だ. なぜだか わからんが, やあいやあい. バア. ベロベロ,

I'm awfully irritated today. | I don't know why, but... | SEE THIS? | BLEHH | NYAH, NYAH!

132

ほくもだ.

Me, too.

トップバッターは
おれだ.

I'm the lead-
off batter.

はじめよう.

Let's
play.

FWOO

ピュッ

めずらしい！
あたったぞ.

Unbelievable!
I hit the ball.

WHOA!

ヒャア

BAP

スコン

なにいってんだ.
うったのはぼくだい.

**YAAY-
YAAY**

Hey, it's
me who
hit the
ball.

ワァ
ワァ

You're
our
hero!

さすが,
ジャイアンくん.

You're terrific,
Gian.

すごい！
ジャイアンくん.

You're
great,
Gian!

われらの英ゆう！

BOFF

よわったな. ぬげない！

My good- ness!

I can't!

まってろ，ぼうしを ぬぐから.

OK, I'll take off my cap.

すみっこに いよう.

あぶない なあ.

I'll get out of here.

It's danger- ous.

TUMP

いたいじゃないか.

Hey! That hurt!

SPISH

SPASH

ドラえもうん，この ぼうしぬがせて.

Doraemon, get it off me!

134

BUMP

あっ,
ドラえもん.

There you are!

WA-A-H

そんなの
いやだあ.

I can't stand it.

ど,
どうしよう.

What should I do?

だれもぼくのこと
かまってくれない…….　もし,
ぼうしが一生ぬげなかったら…….

Nobody cares about me... What if I can't ever take off this cap...?

気にかけられるって,
うれしいねえ.

勉強も
しないで!

なんです. その
かっこうは!

PLOP

And you weren't even studying!

What's that get-up!?

I'm happy they worry about me.

I guess water and sweat made it soft.

水やあせでぬれたので,
ふやけたんだな.

FLIMP

おばあちゃんの
おもいで

Are you tidying up the shed?

ものおきをかたづけているの.

136

Memories of Grandma

ひゃあ. がらくたばかりたまっちゃって.

なつかしいなあ.

This brings back memories.

Wow.

It's filled with junk.

Grandma used to sew him up for me.

He's all patched up!

This was my favorite teddy bear when I was little.

おばあちゃんが, つくろってくれたんだ.

つぎだらけだなあ.

小さいころ, 大好きだった くまちゃんだよ.

だっこされてるのが，のび太くんだね． この人だよ． ぼくがようち園のころ，死んじゃったけどね． おばあちゃんがいたの？

ぼくのこと，すごくかわいがってくれてね． やさしそうな人だ．

そのころからなき虫
だったんだね.

You've been a crybaby since then.

悪かったよ.

もっとすなおにきけ！

I'm sorry.

Just listen to me!

ぼくはおばあちゃんがやさしか
ったという話をしてるんだ.

I'm talking about how gentle Grandma was.

139

SNIFF

I... I...

そうだ.

Hey.

そんな
むりは…….

That's
impossi-
ble...

もういちど，おばあち
ゃんにあいたいよう.

I wish I could
see Grandma
again.

WAAH!

どうして？

そりゃやめた
ほうがいいぞ.

Why?

You'd better
not to
do it.

How will your grandma
feel if she sees you this
grown up?

いきなり大きくなったきみを見たら，
おばあちゃんはどう思う.

「タイムマシン」で，
むかしへ行けばいいんだ.

Let's go back to the
past by "Time
Machine".

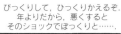

PLUMP

出口が見えてきた.

There's the exit ahead.

あっ, かきの木.

Oh, there's the persimmon tree.

We cut it down the year before last.

おととし
切っちゃったんだ.

わあ, なつかしい
うちの庭だ.

Wow, our dear old yard!

ああ,
そうか.

だれかに見つかるとまずい.
早く, おばあちゃんを見よう.

Oh, you're right.

We don't want to be seen. Let's find her.

家もまだ新しいや.

Our house is so new.

142

おばあちゃんがいつも
いたへやはあっちだよ.

うら口から,
しのびこもう.

Grandma's room is over there.

We'll use the back way.

いいかい, そうっと
のぞくんだ.

Just a peek, remember?

OK.

B-BMP B-BMP B-BMP

SLLLZ

う, うん.

B-BMP B-BMP

いないよ.

……あれ?

She's not here.

...Oh?

いない.

じゃあ, きっと洋間だ.

She's not here.

I'm sure she's in the Western-style room.

このドアはむかしから
たてつけが悪かった.

2階かな.

CLUMP!

ひいてもだめなら
おしてみな.

でも，やがて小じわ
だらけになるけどね.
あら，
そうかしら.
やあっ，やっぱり
わかいなあ！
だ，だれです，
あんたたち.

なんです！よits家に,
だまってはいりこんで!!

おばあちゃん，どこかへ
でかけてるらしいや．

わかるわけ
ないさ．

ぼくだってこと，
わからないのかな．

It looks like Grandma's going out.

Of course, she can't.

How couldn't she recognize her son?

3つのときの
ぼくだ．

あっ．

It's me at the age of 3.

Oh!

いまはにくたら
しいけど．

かわいい
なあ．

WAAH

ワーン

He's cheeky now.

He's lovely.

BOP   BAP

スネ夫とジャイアンの
やつめ！

ゴチ   ゴチ

Suneo and Gian!!

145

こいつら、きのうも学校で、
ぼくをつっころばしたんだ。

よせ、
そんな小さい子を。

よくも、
ぼくをいじめたなっ。

むかしと今をごっちゃに
しちゃだめだい。

146

町じゅうのおもちゃ屋さんをさがしたんだけ
どね. 花火は夏しか売ってないんだって.

ごめんよ.

おばあちゃん,
花火かってきてくれた？

I searched all
the toyshops
in the town,

but they sold
fireworks only
in summer.

I'm
sorry.

Grandma, did
you buy me
fireworks?

はいはい.

おばあちゃんきらいだ.
あっちへいけっ.

いやだい, いやだい,
花火がほしいんだい.

OK,
OK.

I hate you,
Grandma. Go
away!

No, no, I want
fireworks!

WAAAH

こらぼく！おばあちゃんをいじめるな.

Hey, little kid! Don't
bully your grandma.

こ, これには
深いわけが….

あ, あ…,
あのですね.

どうして, うちののび太を
いじめるんです.

I have a good
reason for
this...

W,
Well...

Why did you make
my Nobita cry?

147

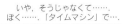

いいえ.

ここへ，へんな子が
きませんでした？

No.

Has a strange boy been in here?

きみが悪いわね.

This is creepy.

また，あの子が？

That boy, again?

いいえ.

おばあちゃんはぼくの
ことあやしまないの.

No.

Gramma, don't you doubt me?

交番へとどけ
たほうがいい
かしら.

Should I call the police?

どこへ，かくれた
のかしら.

Where is he hiding?

Thank you.

ありがとう.

ええ，ええ，
そりゃもう.

Oh yes, very much.

のび太くんが
かわいい？

Do you love Nobita?

おばあ
ちゃん.

Gramma.

149

わたしももう，
年だから．

I'm getting old.

そうもいかない
だろうね．

That's impossible.

いつまでも，いつまでも，
あの子のそばにいてせわを
してあげたいけど，

I want to be with him and take care of him forever, but...

ランドセルしょって，
学校へ行くすがた…．

The sight of his going to school with a satchel on his back...

せめて，小学校へ行くころまで
生きられればいいんだけどね．

I want to live at least until he goes to grade school.

そ，そんなさびしいこと，
いわないでよ．

Please don't, it makes me sad.

ちょっと待ってて！

Wait a minute!

ひと目見たいねえ．

I wish I could see that.

ランドセル！

My satchel!

150

さっきから，なんとなく
そんな気がしてましたよ．

やっぱり
そうかい．

ぼく，のび太です．

信じられないかも
しれないけど．

I've thought so since a little while ago.

Just as I thought.

I'm Nobita.

You won't believe this, but...

OH, GRAMMA

だれが，のびちゃんの
いうこと，うたがう
ものですか．

信じて
くれるの？

うたがわない？

Who would doubt what you say?

You don't doubt me?

Do you believe me?

ねえ，今すぐぼくと
けっこんしてよ．

だめ？

のびちゃんの小学生すがたを
見たら，よくが出ちゃったよ．

You can't?

Can you marry me right now?

I'm happy I could see you as a grade school student. And next,

I want to see your bride.

あんたのおよめさんを，
ひと目見たいねえ．

てんとう虫コミックス「ドラえもん」第4巻 収録作品

英語力を高める ワンポイントレッスン

このコミックでは、意味がわかりやすく、そしてふだんよく使われる英語表現を選んで使用しています。ここでは、さらに英語の理解を深めるために、いくつかの英語表現について例をあげてご説明します。

12ページ2段目

な.

頭悪いな.

He is.

He's kind of slow, isn't he.

ぼくはまだ子どもだぞ. 子どもにまごがあるもんか.

I'm still a child. A child can't have a grandson.

kind of...は口語的表現で、「やや…だ」の意味です。He is slow.「彼は頭が悪い」を「ちょっと頭が悪い」というように、表現を和らげています。

17ページ1段目

こんなまっくろにしなくてもいいだろ.

You've gone too far.

「やりすぎる」と言うときには、go too farを使います。「ちょっとやりすぎる」なら、go a little too farとか、go a bit too farとなります。この言い方は、92、96、99ページにも出てきます。

19ページ3段目

ぼくはもう，生きているのがいやになっちゃった．

I'm sick and tired of life.

ぼ，ぼくは……

I, I...

sick and tired of...は、「…にあきあきして、…にまったくうんざりして」を表す口語表現です。sick of...でも意味は同じですが、sick and tired of...のほうが「いやになった」感じが強調されます。のび太くんのなみだ顔で、よくわかりますね。

21ページ2段目

どこでもいいんだよ．

ちょっと，つけどころがちがうんじゃない？

Anywhere will do.

Hey, isn't it on the wrong place?

このdoは、「役に立つ、十分だ」という意味になります。この意味では、ふつうwillといっしょに使います。

33ページ2段目

十一月ごろ．

Around November.

When is that?

すずしくなるって，いつごろだ．

このaroundは、アメリカの口語表現で「約…」「だいたい…」の意味です。About November.と、aboutを使うこともできます。

42ページ4段目

なんとかして！

もうすぐ時間が
きれる.

Do something!

We're running out of time.

run out of...は、「…がなくなる、…を使い果たす」という意味ですが、今もだんだんなくなってきているので、be running out of...と進行形を使っています.

46ページ2段目

学園祭の打ち合わせ
があるんだぞ.

しずちゃんとこ
へ行く約束だろ.

You've got a school festival planning meeting.

You were supposed to go to the Shizu-chan's house.

be supposed to...は、ふつう「…することになっている」と訳しますが、「…しないのはまずいよ」というニュアンスをふくんでいます。

51ページ1段目

ハハハ, 通信ぼが, オール5だったらという
話さ. そんなこと, ありっこないじゃないか.

Ha, ha, ha, I'll keep my promise if he gets straight A's in his report card. That's impossible.

PHEW!

アメリカでは、成績でいちばん良いのはAなので、「オール5」はstraight A'sと言います。Aがずらっとならんでいるという感じです。

154

68ページ3段目

かるい, かるい.

すごい, ぴったりよ.

It's a piece of cake.

Gee! Perfect!

a piece of cakeは口語表現です。「楽勝だ」「朝めし前だ」というくだけた感じがでます。言葉どうり訳すと、「それはひと切れのケーキです」。これでは意味が通じませんね。

70ページ4段目

ぐるじい〜.

なにがなんでも, ぜんぶたべさせる.

Help me!

I'll make you eat all of them at any cost.

「なにがなんでも」「どうしても」と言うときに使う決まり文句が、at any costです。at all costsも同じように使えます。

75ページ4段目

きっと病院だよ.

うそうそ！

WAAH

Probably they're at the hospital.

I'm kidding!

このkidは、「子ども」ではありません。動詞で「からかう」「じょうだんを言う」の意味になる口語表現です。I'm not kidding.と否定文なら、「じょうだんではないよ」「マジだってば」ということです。

80ページ2段目

きみににたら，成せき
ゆうしゅううたがいなし！

If he takes after you, he's sure to be smart!

take after...は、「…に似る」という意味ですが、特に親の特ちょうに似る場合に使います。その特ちょうとは、姿、形、動作、性格などをさしています。

97ページ2段目

つい，本気にしちゃった．ふしぎだな.　はじめに，うそだとことわっておいたのに….

I took it seriously in spite of myself. Why?

I told you beforehand that it was going to be a lie...

in spite of oneselfは、「（そんなつもりはないのに）つい…してしまう」というときに使う決まり文句です。

113ページ4段目

そろそろ，せんたくものが
かわいたころね.

It's about time the washing dried.

「…してもいいころだ」を表すit's about time...を使っています。…の部分の動詞が、driedと過去形になるのがポイントです。

127ページ1段目

あぶないっ。おちたらどうするの！

とてもよく使う表現のwatch outです。「気をつける」「用心する」という意味で、ほとんどの場合命令形で使います。「車に気をつけなさい」なら、Watch out for cars.のように言うことができます。

137ページ2段目

おばあちゃんが，つくろってくれたんだ.

つぎはぎだらけだなあ.

used to...は「昔はよく…したものだった」と過去の習慣を表します。「…するようなことはなかった」と否定文にするには、Grandma used not to sew him up for me.のように、usedとtoの間にnotを入れます。

140ページ3段目

どうして？

そりゃやめたほうがいいぞ.

'd better...は、had better...の省略した形で「…したほうがよい」「…するべきだ」を表します。ここではnotを使って否定文にしていますから、「…しないほうがよい」「…するのはまずい」となります。

DORAEMON

既刊 ①〜⑩巻 定価：本体780円+税

てんとう虫コミックス「ドラえもん」の1巻から31巻までを収録。
DORAEMONイングリッシュ・コミックは、すべて収録している
ストーリーが異なるので、重複する話はありません。
どの巻からでも安心してお楽しみください。

©藤子プロ・小学館

- 悪運ダイヤ
- 人間機関車
- マッチ売りのドラえもん
- オトコンナを飲めば？
- 消しゴムで
  ノッペラボウ
- ロボットがほめれば…
- ジーンと感動する話
- ひっこし地図
- トレーサーバッヂ
- テンテンハウスは
  気楽だな
- おそだアメ
- アパートの木
- いないいないシャワー
- たとえ胃の中、水の中
- のび太の恐竜

- さいなんくんれん機
- 雲の中の散歩
- おおかみ男クリーム
- おすそわけガム
- さいみんグラス
- あらかじめアンテナ
- とりよせバッグ
- ミサイルが追ってくる
- ウラオモテックス
- わすれ鳥
- カミナリになれよう
- ゆうれいの干物
- 大男がでたぞ
- 手にとり望遠鏡
- 弓やで学校へ
- マジックハンド
- タマシイム・マシン
- 立体コピー

- ふくびんコンビ
- ゴルゴンの首
- ツモリガン
- 宇宙探検すごろく
- ココロコロン
- 雪山のロマンス
- ドラキュラセット
- 念写カメラマン
- 精霊よびだしうてわ
- しつけキャンディー
- 無事故でけがをした話
- ラジコンシミュレーターで
  ぶっとばせ
- デビルカード
- のび太救出決死探検隊
- オモイコミン

- 本人ビデオ
- もはん手紙ペン
- おそるべき正義ロープ
- おざしき水族館
- 忘れ物おくりとどけ機
- ほくよりダメな
  やつがきた
- おかし牧場
- めだちライトで人気者
- ジャイアンリサイタルを
  楽しむ方法
- のび太のなが〜い家出
- まんが家ジャイ子
- な、なんと！
  のび太が100点とった!!
- カンヅメカンでまんがを
- のび太の結婚前夜

SHOGAKUKAN ENGLISH COMICS

DORAEMON

Doraemon ①
SHOGAKUKAN ENGLISH COMICS

デザイン／海野一雄＋ベイブリッジ・スタジオ
カバーイラスト／むぎわらしんたろう ©藤子プロ
英訳・編集協力／(株)ジャレックス
英訳協力／VIZ Media,LLC
協力／(株)小学館集英社プロダクション

2002年3月20日　初版第1刷発行
2017年11月21日　　　第27刷発行

著　者	藤 子・F・不 二 雄
	©藤 子 プ ロ
発行者	杉　本　　　隆
印刷所	文唱堂印刷株式会社
製本所	株式会社　難波製本

PRINTED IN JAPAN

発行所　(〒101-8001)東京都千代田区一ツ橋二の三の一　株式会社 小学館
　　　　TEL　販売03(5281)3555　編集03(3230)9349

ISBN4-09-227011-9